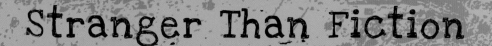

WILD ANIMALS

By Virginia Loh-Hagan

Disclaimer: This series focuses on the strangest of the strange. Have fun reading about strange people and things! But please do not try any of the antics in this book. Be safe and smart!

45th Parallel Press

Published in the United States of America by Cherry Lake Publishing
Ann Arbor, Michigan
www.cherrylakepublishing.com

Reading Adviser: Marla Conn MS, Ed., Literacy specialist, Read-Ability, Inc.
Book Designer: Melinda Millward

Photo Credits: © Kerryn Parkinson/ NORFANZ/ZUMA Press/Newscom, cover, 11; © Jarous/Shutterstock.com, 1; © traveler1116/ iStockphoto, 5; © Seth LaGrange/Shutterstock.com, 6; © SteveByland/iStockphoto, 7; © Rusty Dodson | Dreamstime.com, 8; © natchapohn/Shutterstock.com, 10; © DANUN/Shutterstock.com, 12; © Jana Shea/Shutterstock.com, 13; © Klaus/http:// www.flickr.com/ CC BY-SA 2.0, 14; © JohnCarnemolla/iStockphoto, 15; © Kathryn Scott Osler/The Denver Post/Getty Images, 16; © Kaliva/Shutterstock.com, 18; © Tony Magdaraog/Shutterstock.com, 19; © Neal Krummell/http://www.flickr.com/ CC BY-SA 2.0, 2; © brownpau/http://www.flickr.com/ CC-BY-2.0, 21; © Sprocky/Shutterstock.com, 22; © Trahcus/Shutterstock. com, 23; © PAUL NICKLEN/National Geographic Creative, 25; © Malchev/iStockphoto, 26; © ASSOCIATED PRESS, 27; © MR1805/Thinkstock, 28; © Goriachikh Oksana/Shutterstock.com, 30; © Europics/Newscom, 31

Graphic Element Credits: ©saki80/Shutterstock.com, back cover, front cover, multiple interior pages; ©queezz/Shutterstock. com, back cover, front cover, multiple interior pages; ©Ursa Major/Shutterstock.com, front cover, multiple interior pages; ©Zilu8/Shutterstock.com, multiple interior pages

45th Parallel Press is an imprint of Cherry Lake Publishing.

Library of Congress Cataloging-in-Publication Data has been filed and is available at catalog.loc.gov

Printed in the United States of America
Corporate Graphics

About the Author

Dr. Virginia Loh-Hagan is an author, university professor, former classroom teacher, and curriculum designer. She thinks her dog, Woody, is strange. He might be part-cat, part-goat, and part-T-Rex. She lives in San Diego with her very tall husband and very naughty dogs. To learn more about her, visit www.virginialoh.com.

Table of Contents

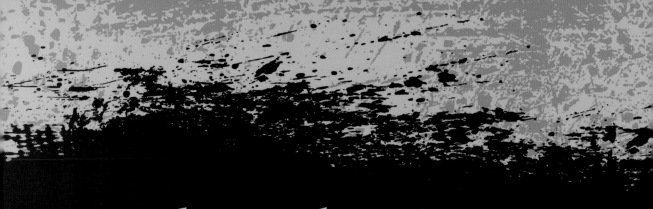

Introduction

Many animals live in this world. They live in different places. They live on land. They live in the sea. Some fly in the air. They do different things to survive. Survive means to stay alive. They eat other animals. They're eaten by other animals. Their bodies are built for their habitats. Habitats are where they live.

There are many types of animals. Some are stranger than others. They look strange. They act strange. But there's strange. And then there's really strange. These stories are hard to believe. They sound like fiction. But they're all true!

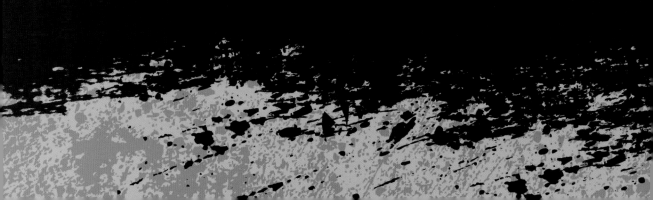

Some animals are wild. Some are tame.

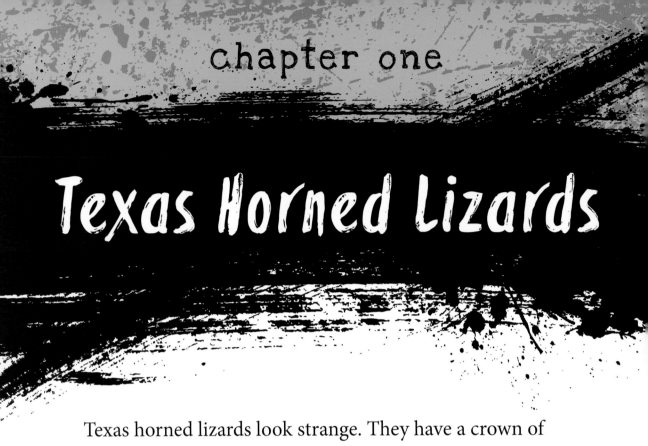

chapter one

Texas Horned Lizards

Texas horned lizards look strange. They have a crown of horns. They puff up. They look really fat. They look like a spiky balloon. Their scales stick out. This makes them hard to swallow. This keeps **predators** away. Predators are hunters.

Their eyes shoot blood. They have **ducts** in the corners of their eyes. Ducts are like tubes. The ducts close up when the lizard is threatened. This stops the blood flowing in their heads. They swell up. The blood pressure increases. Then, the ducts burst. The blood can shoot 5 feet (1.5 meters). They blind predators. Predators get confused. This gives lizards time to run away.

Horned lizards' blood tastes gross.

Eastland County is in Texas. In 1897, it opened a new courthouse. People heard lizards slept for 100 years. They tested this idea. They buried a live lizard. They put it in the main stone of the courthouse. The lizard was buried for 31 years.

In 1928, people opened the stone. The lizard looked dead. Someone held it. It came to life! People were shocked. Some didn't believe it. They thought it was a joke.

The lizard was named "Old Rip." Rip became famous. Then it got sick. It died a year later. People stuffed its body. It's on show at the courthouse. In 1973, someone stole it. It was later found.

Horned lizards sit in the sun.

Explained by Science

A squitten is a strange cat. It has short arms. This makes it look like a squirrel. Some people think it's a kitten and squirrel combined. But it's not. It's a mutant. Its short arms are due to a mistake. All living things have cells. These cells have a specific order. The order forms a code. This code tells cells what to do. Sometimes, the cells get out of order. Sometimes, the cells break. Sometimes, the cells change. This all causes mutations. Mutations are nature's mistakes. Some mutations create interesting animals. Being strange makes some mutants special.

chapter two

Blobfish

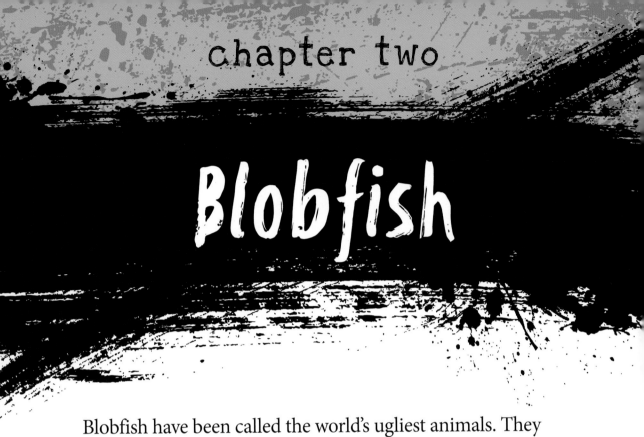

Blobfish have been called the world's ugliest animals. They live deep in the ocean. They live near Australia. Their skin looks like jelly. It looks like goo. It helps them survive. It helps them float. Blobfish don't have to swim. This saves energy. They don't have muscle. They eat whatever floats in front of them. They have droopy mouths. They have blobby cheeks.

Mr. Blobby is the most famous blobfish. It's dead. It's kept in a jar like pickles. It's studied by scientists. Its picture was taken. Mr. Blobby became a star. It has followers on social media. It

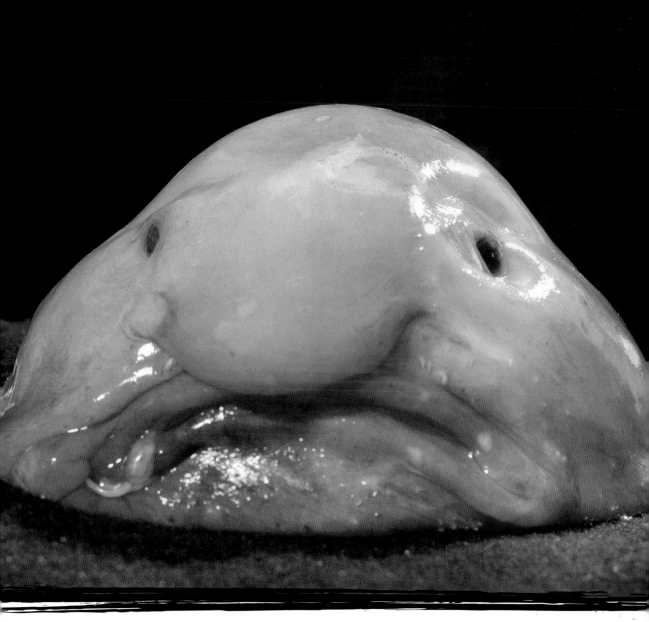

Out of water, blobfish are limp and flabby.
They can't support their own weight.

was on TV. It inspired plush toys. It inspired games.
It inspired songs.

chapter three

Horseshoe Crabs

Horseshoe crabs look like aliens. They're older than dinosaurs. They're also not crabs. They're more like spiders. They have 12 legs. They have 10 eyes. They can see light that humans can't see. And their blood is special. It's baby blue! It protects them. It traps germs. Germs can't spread. People use their blood to test drugs. Their blood is used to test for bad germs. Their blood saves people's lives.

Horseshoe crabs are collected from beaches. They're taken to special labs. They're cleaned. Their blood is taken. They're returned to the beach. One quart (1 liter) of their blood is $15,000.

Horseshoe crabs are over 450 million years old.

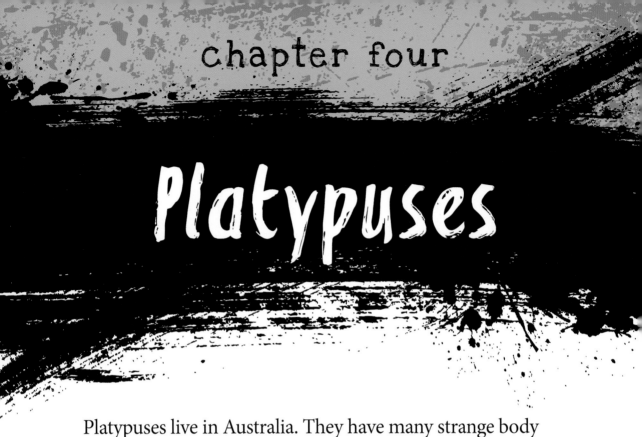

chapter four

Platypuses

Platypuses live in Australia. They have many strange body parts. They have duck **bills**. Bills are beaks. They have mole bodies. They have beaver tails. They have otter feet.

Males have another special body part. They have sharp stingers. Stingers are on their back feet. They have poison.

A platypus was brought to Great Britain in 1799. This was the first time people there saw a platypus. They didn't believe it. They thought they were being tricked. They thought someone had sewn animal parts together. The platypus

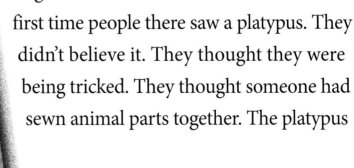

Platypuses are special mammals. They lay eggs.

seemed too strange to be real. This is because people
have sewn animals together before.

Fishermen around the Fiji islands sewed animals together. They sewed monkeys and fish together. Samuel Barrett Edes was an American sea captain. He bought one of these creatures. He brought it to the United States. It became known as the Feejee Mermaid. It had a monkey's head and body. It had a fish tail. It was shown in a circus museum.

Scientists sewed two mice together. They sewed a young mouse to an old mouse. The young mouse pumped young blood into the old mouse. The young blood made the old mouse more active. It also created new brain cells.

The Feejee Mermaid was in P. T. Barnum's circus museum.

Spotlight Biography

Tom Leppard was also known as Leopard Man. (His real name was Tom Woodbridge.) He lived in Scotland. He had a world record. He was the world's most tattooed man. He tattooed his skin. He made himself look like a leopard. He even lived like a leopard. He lived in a small hut. He lived far away from town. His floor was the dirt ground. His roof was a metal sheet. His bed was a foam board. He cooked on a small stove. He didn't have electricity. He didn't have a phone. He didn't have TV. He used a small boat to go to town. He picked up supplies.

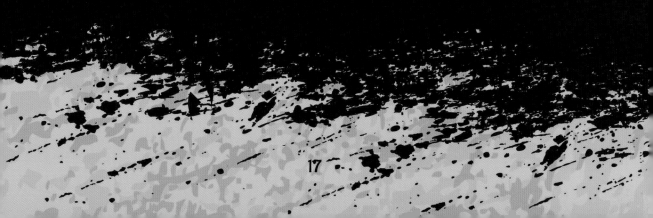

chapter five

Octogoat

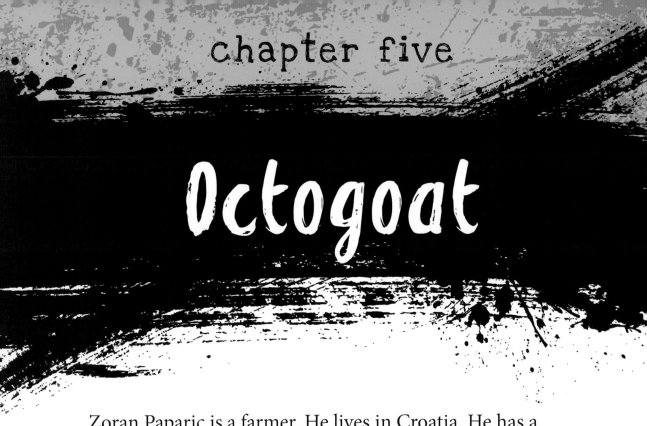

Zoran Paparic is a farmer. He lives in Croatia. He has a goat. The goat's name is Sarka. Sarka had **kids**. Kids are baby goats. Most of the kids were normal. But one was not. This kid had eight legs. It had both male and female parts.

Paparic was shocked. He said, "I thought I was seeing things. Then I called my neighbor to make sure that I am not crazy." But his eyes weren't tricking him. The kid was named Octogoat. Octogoat couldn't walk. It couldn't stand.

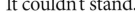

Sometimes animals are born with extra parts. This cow has too many legs.

Animal doctors checked Octogoat. They said it had a twin. The twin didn't grow properly. Octogoat absorbed the twin in the womb.

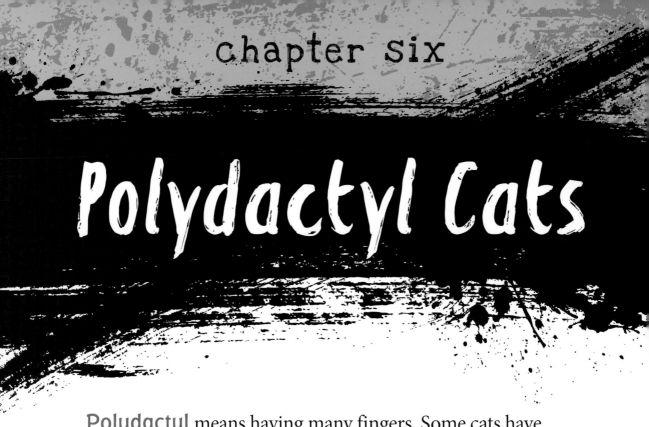

chapter six

Polydactyl Cats

Polydactyl means having many fingers. Some cats have many toes. They use their extra toes. They open windows. They open locks.

Ernest Hemingway was a famous author. He loved cats. A sea captain gave him a cat with six toes. This happened in the 1930s. Hemingway loved the cat. He named it Snowball. Sixty cats still live in Hemingway's house. Half of these cats have extra toes. They're related to Snowball. This is why polydactyl cats are sometimes called "Hemingway cats."

President Theodore Roosevelt had a polydactyl cat. Its name was Slippers.

Jake is a cat. It lives in Canada. It was a world record. It has 28 toes. Seven toes are on each paw.

chapter seven

Snakes

Snakes have a strong bite **reflex**. A reflex is a quick movement. Snakes just bite once. They bite quickly. Then, they move away. Their bites take less than a second.

So, it's strange for a snake's **prey** to get away. This rarely happens. Prey are animals hunted for food.

A big snake ate a little snake. It swallowed it whole. A pet cat killed the big snake. The little snake escaped. It wriggled its way out of the big snake. The cat's owner took pictures. This happened in Greece. This happened in 2011.

Snakes usually swallow prey's heads first.

chapter eight

Narwhals

A Danish throne was made of "unicorn horns." Queen Elizabeth I had a "unicorn horn." But these were all fakes. The horns were actually narwhal **tusks**. Tusks are teeth that are like horns.

Narwhals are whales. They live in the Arctic waters. Male narwhals have one extended tusk. (Some females have it. But their tusks are smaller. They're less spiraled.) The tusk shoots out from the mouth. It's spiraled. It's made of ivory. It keeps growing. It's between 5 and 10 feet (1.5 and 3 m) long. It's hollow. It weighs about 22 pounds (10 kilograms). It has a lot of nerves. It's sensitive. One in 500 males has two tusks.

Narwhals are the unicorns of the sea.

chapter nine

Cyclops Albino Shark

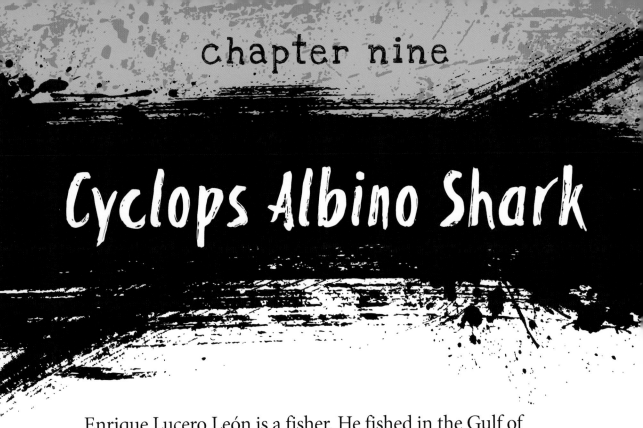

Enrique Lucero León is a fisher. He fished in the Gulf of California. He caught a dusky shark. The shark was **pregnant**. Pregnant means it's carrying a baby. León cut open the shark. He found several baby sharks. But one baby shark was strange. It was **albino**. Albino means all white. It also had one eye. The eye was large. It was at the front of its head.

Scientists studied the shark. They confirmed it was a cyclops shark. There aren't many cyclops sharks in the world. None have been caught outside the womb. A scientist said, "This is extremely rare."

26

Less than 50 examples of sharks with one eye have been recorded.

Cyclopia is a condition. It's when animals are born with one eye. This is a birth defect. The brain failed to separate into two parts. Only one eye is formed. Animals with cyclopia don't live long. If they're born, they'd have a hard time surviving in the wild.

Sharks must be strong the minute they're born. Cyclops sharks can't protect themselves. They'd be helpless. They'd die.

Other animals became famous for having one eye. Cy was a cyclops kitten. It had one eye. It didn't have an eyelid. It didn't have a nose. It only lived one day.

Cyclops are giants with one eye. They come from Greek myths.

Try This!

- Visit a zoo. Make a list of new animals that you saw. Take pictures of them. Learn more about these animals.

- Help out at a local animal shelter. Walk dogs. Feed animals. Clean cages. Help promote the adoption of shelter pets.

- Watch an animal. Study its habits. Study its actions. Make notes about it. See if the animal does anything strange. (Scientists study animals in their natural homes.)

- Adopt a pet. (Get permission from your parents.) Take care of the pet. Love the pet.

- Watch YouTube videos about animals. Find the strangest-looking animal. Find the strangest-acting animal.

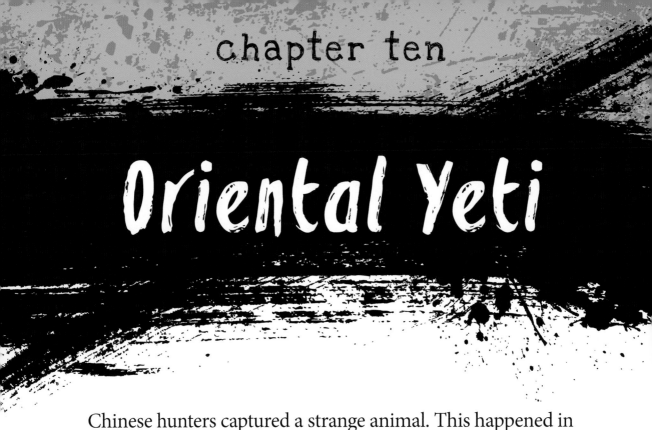

chapter ten
Oriental Yeti

Chinese hunters captured a strange animal. This happened in 2010. No one knew what the animal was. It's been called the "**Oriental** yeti." Oriental means Asian things. A yeti is a **mythical** monster. Mythical means there are stories about it.

The animal looked a bit like a bear. But it didn't have any fur. It had a tail like a kangaroo. It sounded like a cat. It was in poor shape. It had sores on its skin.

Some scientists think it was a sick **civet**. Civets are catlike creatures. Some scientists

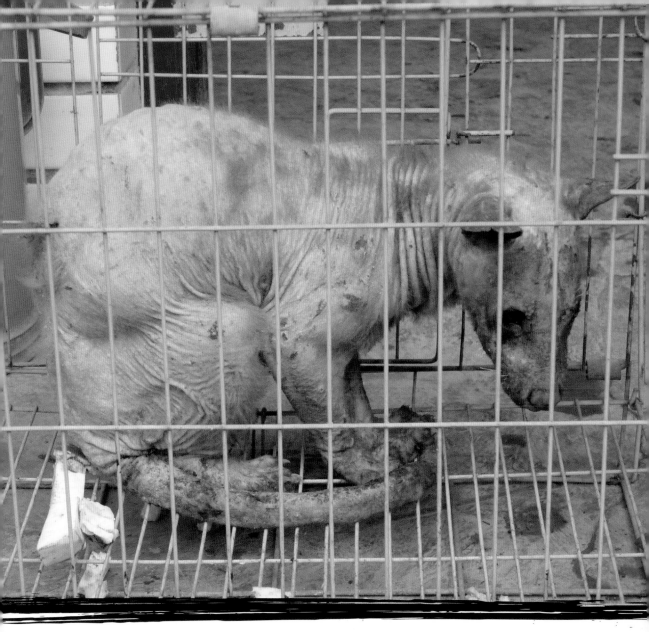

People have been looking for the Oriental yeti for years.

think the animal was shaved. They think it was a trick.
No one has seen the animal again.

Consider This!

Take a Position! Some people try to make new animals. They breed two different animals together. What do you think about this? Should this practice be allowed? Argue your point with reasons and evidence.

Say What? Research a "strange" animal. Describe the animal. Explain what makes the animal strange.

Think About It! Early explorers were confused by animals. They created stories to explain unfamiliar animals. For example, sailors saw manatees. Manatees were strange to them. The sailors thought the manatees were mermaids. Create a story to explain an unfamiliar animal.

Learn More!

- Ghigna, Charles. *Strange, Unusual, Gross & Cool Animals*. New York: Liberty Street, 2016.
- Polydoros, Lori. *Strange but True Animals*. North Mankato, MN: Capstone Press, 2010.
- Spelman, Lucy. *Animal Encyclopedia: 2,500 Animals with Photos, Maps, and More!* Washington, DC: National Geographic, 2012.

Glossary

albino (al-BYE-noh) having no pigment, being all white

bills (BILZ) flat beaks

civet (SIH-vit) catlike mammals that live in Africa and Asia

cyclopia (sye-KLO-pee-uh) condition of being born with one eye

ducts (DUHKTS) tubes, vessels

habitats (HAB-uh-tats) environments where animals live

kids (KIDZ) baby goats

mythical (MITH-ih-kuhl) legendary, being told in stories or myths

Oriental (or-ee-EN-tuhl) Asian thing

polydactyl (pah-lee-DAK-tuhl) having many fingers or toes

predators (PRED-uh-turz) hunters

pregnant (PREG-nuhnt) carrying a baby

prey (PRAY) animals hunted for food

reflex (REE-fleks) quick reaction or movement

survive (sur-VIVE) to stay alive

tusks (TUHSKS) long teeth coming out of the mouth

Index